Understanding Genocide: Inter-generational Abstraction and Dilution Through Three Generations Grappling with The Holocaust

By Eden Mia Hoffman

First printing, 2018.

ISBN: 9781983173783
Imprint: Independently published

Dedicated to those who perished, those who persisted, and those who propel us forward.

"For the dead and the living, we must bear witness."
- Eli Wiesel

A Note on the Holocaust and Genocide

The International Holocaust Remembrance Alliance recently published a Working Paper drafted by the Committee on the Holocaust, Genocide and Crimes Against Humanity titled "History Never Repeats Itself, but Sometimes It Rhymes Comparing the Holocaust to Different Atrocities." This builds on an earlier paper by the Education Working Group (EWG), "The Holocaust and Other Genocides," which introduced educators to the idea of comparing the Holocaust to other crimes against humanity. The title of the paper is accurate-- History does not repeat itself, but it can follow similar trajectories. As I weave through time, place and generation in my research endeavor, I would like to qualify my approach to the Holocaust, both on a personal and scholarly level. The Holocaust is by no means identical to any other era, atrocity, locale or regime. The same goes for the Armenian genocide, the My Lai Massacre, Srebrenica, the Rwandan genocide, or any other event for that matter. Furthermore, I strongly contend that no two individuals had the same experience during the war. Every situation was wholly circumstantial, as is every survivor, and their family and coping mechanisms. The aim of this paper is not to generalize, qualify, abstract or make sweeping statements. Rather, it is to explore the ways that the Holocaust is presented by way of intergenerational memory transmission and how places as sites of understanding and commemoration create a critical lens through which contemporary issues can be analyzed.

The history of WWII is, for the most part, known but not understood. History works to serve the present and to make way for the future. The meaning of the past is created by the present; so, to look at how the Holocaust is presented today, and how the third generation, in particular, looks to this epoch, leads to a certain relationship and understanding of contemporary time. Mobilizing this use of history as a critical lens for looking at, understanding, and most importantly, acting, can create change and fulfill the message of "Never Again." An apprehension of the presentation of the Holocaust today for the younger generations is important to analyze; however, where do we go from there? Do we present the facts, provide evidence and testimony? What happens when museums cannot fully fulfill that role, or when survivors are dying out? What is the mission of the museum in creating change in the world today, and for the future? Is it enough?

My strong sense of urgency for a grasp on current perspectives of genocides and crimes against humanity stems from the waves of terror that have rocked the world in recent years, the current events in Syria and Africa, the absence of an interdisciplinary approach of understanding history and the venomous buzz words flying around the political realm (e.g. "evil", "Holocaust", "dictatorship", "manipulation", "marginalize" etc.). But, the most compelling reason for me to study this topic, at this specific time and place, is the sheer fact that survivors are dying out. The cycle of life comes with memories, and as time goes on and people change, so too, the memories they carry. When our first-hand witnesses, survivors and warriors, are no longer, we must do everything in our power to give their memories life, and to carry them on, because if we don't, then who will?

Postmemory and the Third Generation

In September of 2016 I started to visit a Holocaust survivor in Brooklyn bi-weekly. Originally, I thought this was going to be routine—every week I would go to her apartment for at least an hour and she would tell me her story. That was not what happened.

This was not going to be my first-time hearing from a Holocaust survivor, but it would be my first time in a one-on-one, intimate setting. While I grew up with the horrors of the Holocaust lingering in the background of my classroom studies, friend's familial backgrounds and community commemoration ceremonies every year, I did not read Holocaust memoirs, watch documentaries or study that era for the fear of having nightmares. I was simultaneously exposed, and shielded, as a child growing up in the third generation. I never sought to delve deeper into the nightmarish stories or to hear more about the horrors of the camps. What I knew (which barely even skimmed the surface) was already enough to shake me. Then, my senior year of high school, while on a trip to Prague with my family I visited Theresienstadt. Three months later I went to Washington, D.C. to the United States Holocaust Memorial

Museum for the first time. And three months after that I visited the History Museum at Yad Vashem in Jerusalem, Israel for the first time as an adult. Here was a shift, it was me going further into this time, learning more and seeing more, understanding a tiny bit more and looking at the Holocaust with a different set of eyes. Each museum was completely different, architecturally, contextually, geographically, historically. I began to attend speaker events with survivors of the Holocaust a bit more frequently, and I even sought an opportunity to spend time weekly at Yad Vashem during a gap year I spent in Israel.

So, during my junior year at NYU, when I heard about the chance to take a social work course where students visited a Holocaust survivor weekly, I decided that this was a great way for me to have the pressure of a weekly visit, rather than attempting to make plans on my own. I needed the pressure, I wanted the pressure, and I surely felt the pressure. This was 2016, seventy-plus years after the Holocaust. Survivors were growing older, and I recognized the unfortunate fact that this would not be an opportunity for much longer. Even if I wasn't ready, I realized I never would be. This was a traumatic subject, but something I felt I had to do.

The first time I called my survivor to schedule a time to come over, I was nervous. The language barrier was hard, and I had no idea what to say. She was excited for me to come visit, so we decided on a day and time and I went. After a few visits, there was still no mention of the Holocaust. I knew that she knew I was coming to spend time with her and to hear her story, but there was just no mention. She often liked to sit by the computer and have us to try to navigate the internet together. One time, we were looking at pictures of the Grand Canyon on the computer, when she suddenly got up and ran to grab a stack of pictures. Every picture was taken at a different place all over the world—Monaco, the Grand Canyon, California, Spain-- and with each one she gave a bit of context in broken English. This was the closest I got to a life story. But, at this point, I approached the visits differently. I was not going to try to find something; I was going because I felt it was important to spend time with this elderly woman. I saw how much she appreciated the visits, and perhaps even the fact that I would come to Brooklyn to sit with her and look up the weather on the computer. I didn't poke with questions, or try to divert from what she wanted to do. I let her call the shots, and I accepted the fact that although I knew she had told her story in the past, she did not want to tell it to me. The memories were hers, and perhaps she was just not ready to share them with me, a stranger.

***

Memory is a vehicle through which we can uncover or restore what otherwise might remain dormant in our historical narrative, but it can also create distance. There is a distinction between authentic memory and postmemory. To engage with the term *postmemory*-- as coined by Marianne Hirsch and Leo Spitzer— is to examine a "consequence of traumatic recall, but at a generational remove." At the fore of 20th and 21st century memory studies are the Holocaust and the guardianship of memory. What do we hold on to from those years, and what do we let go of? How is "the sense of living connection" bound to the three generations post-Holocaust? And, where does the received, transferred knowledge of events lay in the context of "the memory of history" — is it in myth or in memory?

For Hirsch, post memory is not mediated by recall, but rather by creatives acts of transformation, and through imaginative investments. For one to be so deeply connected to a firsthand account—like a testimony from a Holocaust survivor— and to register it is as a memory of their own, is to capture the essence of post memory. Hirsch explains this phenomenon as the quality of the relationship to the memory of the first generation; the transformation of memory not mediated by recall, but rather created as a result of "the transferential process (cognitive and affective) ...internalized without being fully understood." Postmemory challenges the link, it distorts it.   This idea of post is interesting. According to the dictionary, the word "post" is a preposition meaning "subsequent to; after"; it is also a prefix that carries the meaning of "after in time or order." To use the term post is to affirm that there is something prior, something for the post to be affixed to (like a post-it note); it is tangential. So, to use the term post memory is to add another layer onto memory, implying that there must be a foundation of memory already in place for which the subsequent generation affixes their notions, considerations and recall. Hence, to begin to journey down the perceived path of the third generation—and, perhaps, even the fourth—it makes complete sense to arrive from a solid understanding of the first generation of Holocaust survivors.

Postmemory makes identification possible. It is used to fill in the gaps of communication and is typically provoked by a sense of urgency. Periods of silence after the war—whether a public silence, or an individual silence—came to be filled by apparatuses of postmemory, like museums and monuments. But, while postmemory creates a link, it also shields. "In forging a protective shield particular to the post generation, one could say that, paradoxically, they actually reinforce the *living* connection between past and present, between the generation of witnesses and survivors and the generation after," Hirsch explains. As it works to create a connection between the past and the present, postmemory affixes itself to memory while functioning analogously to provide a shield to the trauma as it builds on top of it, creating a new memory, a new connection. Beginning with the post war years (1945-1968), and up until the present today, there is debate about silence during these years. It is believed by a number of historians and residents of that time, that the Holocaust was not spoken about during this time, while others deny this claim. This myth of post war silence came from a generational divide. Whereas many young Americans during that time were looking for problems with the previous generation(s), so too, young Jews living in America during that time looked to the prior generation with careful eyes, analyzing their way of life. The difference here is that these young Jews were mainly the children of survivors, the second generation. This post-generation sought to assert themselves as victims too, which ultimately lead to what Marianne Hirsch coined as "the fantasies of witnessing"— the production of arts to mediate memory. Today, there is no shortage of memorials, lectures, memoirs, exhibitions, artwork and scholarly works that address the Holocaust.

***

On a rather warm day in February, I sat down on a bench on the main level of the United States Holocaust Museum in Washington, D.C. Before I could blink, a gaggle of three middle-school-aged girls came hurrying to the same bench. "No, don't bother her, she just sat down. You have to be quiet here, some people are thinking and she's busy," one girl whispered loudly to another as she approached the bench to sit. I moved over and invited them to share the bench with me as I struck up a brief conversation with them while they waited for the rest of their classmates to finish the exhibit on that floor. I asked them their age and where they were from—fourteen years old and from Virginia, at the museum on a class trip. "Is it your first time here?" I asked, to which they replied "Yes" in unison. They told me that they had been learning about the Holocaust in school and they came to the museum for the day. I asked them what they thought. "Underwhelming" one girl immediately responded, to which I replied by asking what they had seen. "Well we saw the train car upstairs, and there were a lot of pictures. But the whole thing was underwhelming." Before anyone had a chance for the next sentence, the rest of their classmates appeared and they were on their way. I understood the possibility that they could be underwhelmed as a result of a modified tour, or sense of remove from the Holocaust itself, being that none of them were descendants of survivors or had any connection to WWII at all. But, in all honesty, the museum is pretty intense and overwhelming. In a case like this, does the museum itself serve as an apparatus of postmemory? Perhaps for those already familiar (and shall I say traumatized) with the events of the Holocaust, the visual scarring of this trauma comes by way of the museum itself. When I-- a third generation Jew but not a descendant of survivors-- think about the

Holocaust, the visual memory for me comes from an amalgam of books, images, speakers, visits with survivors and mainly, museums.

The middle school children from Virginia and myself are both a part of the third generation, a generation that as a whole constitutes one of postmemory. We simultaneously connect to, and shield ourselves, from this trauma. Two encounters with the Holocaust, two distinct elements of postmemory, two apparatuses of forging a connection, yet for the same generation. I was simultaneously linked and shielded in my encounter as I had a physical link to the Holocaust, a connection with a survivor, but was shielded from her actual story. The schoolchildren were simultaneously shielded and connected to the memory of the Holocaust as they visited a postmemorial site-- a link-- but the encounter left them underwhelmed, and shielded from the trauma, they felt. However, being underwhelmed is different than being disconnected. I may have been underwhelmed from my visits, but I was far from disconnected. A visit to the USHMM was underwhelming for these children, but it did not disconnect them. Quite the contrary; perhaps it actually gave them a sense of connection, and more of a reason to delve deeper, to understand more and to learn more, in order to become overwhelmed and emotionally attached. It is evident from encounters like these that a connection to the Holocaust is not defined by a relationship of transmission. The third (and fourth) generations post-Holocaust is charged with a task. Neither myself or the schoolchildren can be seen as failing that task. Rather, it is these experiences that render it clear that perhaps there are multiple ways to fulfill the task of commemoration, memorialization, transmission and testimony.

How can historical memory be kept from going stale? How can events from decades ago be represented today? How can they be integrated into narratives that make sense to the generations of today, to local audiences whether they have an immediate connection to the Shoah or not? While I've explored an amalgam of opinions, justifications, questions and ideologies, it all seems to boil down to sheer dialogue. The first step to be taken is to talk, and subsequently, to engage. Today, the third (and fourth) generation are most needed, as they are the last ones to be able to hear form survivors firsthand. My children will not be able to hear from a Holocaust survivor at the annual Yom Hashoah Remembrance ceremonies each Spring, nor will I in a few years. This is the sad reality that we live with, and while there is not much left to do in the race against biology, what we can control is the passing down of these stories, the sharing of legacy.

Sites of Postmemory

"We live in a historical age that calls out for memory because it has abandoned it" Pierre Nora wrote in 1989. "Museums, archives, cemeteries, festivals, anniversaries, treaties, depositions, monuments, sanctuaries, fraternal orders—these are the boundary stones of another age, illusions of eternity." *Lieux de memoire* (sites of memory) are how Nora refers to these efforts of immortality, because "without commemorative vigilance, history would soon sweep them away." Pierre Nora wrote this is in 1989, insinuating a sense of urgency. Today, in 2017, there is a sense of urgency like no other. In a few years, survivors will no longer be living. We need these monuments and memorials to grasp their memories and engage with them, to run with them and use them to educate, to prevent, to remember, to memorialize and to actively combat the threat of "never again." Physical images and tangible sites help historical memory from going stale. Yet, they do more than that. Primo Levi, the Jewish Italian chemist and survivor of Auschwitz contrasts the recounting of perception and photographs from Auschwitz, because "if we came back home and wanted to tell, we would be missing the words." Photographs, on the other hand, "demonstrate what information theory claims: that an image, parity of scale, 'tells' twenty, one hundred times more." "More and better than the word, they recapture the impression which the camps, well or badly preserved, more or less transformed into grand sites and sanctuaries, make on the visitor; an impression that is strangely deeper and more unsettling for those who have never been there than on us few survivors." *Lieux de memoire* establish memory for those who haven't witnessed it firsthand. It then becomes their burden, an eerie sense of traumatic recall, a part of them. A great concern of the earlier centuries was how to mobilize and monumentalize the past in order to establish these events as legitimate, and thus, to attribute meaning to the present in order to envision the future. As urban spaces emerged, they took on significance as they "represented the material traces of the historical past in the present." As a result of technology, boundaries between the past and present have changed, and are no longer strong bonds, rather times meshing into each other. Palimpsests, as Andreas Huyssen explains, are what cities and buildings have become and are "the strong marks of present space. … Representations of the visual will always show residues of traces of the invisible.""" Museums and monuments are human attempts to transcend time, increasingly evident today as "modernity has brought with it a very real compression of time and space." Different media of memory aid in public memory as well, allowing people to break out of traumatic remembrances and combatting the threat of socially produced amnesia, a threat particularly evident as survivors and first-hand witnesses are dying out. "At stake in our current history/memory debate is not only a disturbance of our notions of the past, but a fundamental crisis in our imagination of alternative futures," Huyssen explains. Memory is hard to grasp; huge parts of it can easily slip away and cannot be regained. Spaces as palimpsests, both on a personal and collective level, are a way in which the past can serve the present, and even the future.

Often, the atrocities of this time period are unfamiliar terrain, perhaps read about in a history textbook or encountered in a memoir. They are abstracted, especially as time moves on and we find ourselves further away from the event itself. However, at the same time, many commentators now refer to a "memory boom", that began in the 1970's and unwound through the turn of the century. This dilution of memory and "Holocaust tourism" that many speak of, stems from the same periods where postmemory began to appear, as it sought to save and transmit the experience of the Holocaust. These tours, like March of the Living, are made to establish a connection of survivors and subsequent generations with an unknown place or identity. Therefore, postmemory and collective identity are foundational to this boom of memory studies, but are not unique to it. During this era, we saw major landmarks—like the *Holocaust* TV miniseries (1979), Steven Spielberg's *Schindler's List* (1993) and Claude Landsman's *Shoah* (1985)—matched by other forms of intellectual confrontation in the form of documentary and music. Video testimonies, archives, museums and monuments, documentation collections, school curricula and pilgrimage tourist sites saw huge numbers of visitors, especially with the advent of new media and the birth of a third generation—those who were neither the survivors nor the children of survivors. The proliferation of these sites has given rise to the memory boom, perhaps diluting it, but it has also allowed the unengaged to become educated and aware.

Anne Frank, the popular "image of the Holocaust" has, and continues to be, the subject of exhibitions, books and shows around the globe—not to mention a tourist site as well. In the past decade, we've seen an influx of visitors flocking to the Anne Frank house in Amsterdam and huge numbers reading her diary. However, similar to the way the contemporary Yiddishists—like Nathan Englander-- use the Holocaust as an identity tool, they also use this public figure of Anne Frank as an access point. Both affiliated and non-affiliated Jews address this with different viewpoints. "Within the Jewish community, there is an urge to detract [from Anne Frank], this idea of giving voice to voiceless. Holocaust museums give cards with random names [to the visitor] so that they are able to connect to random person and follow their story throughout their experience," Jessie Mayer, a researcher on contemporary Yiddishists, explains. On the contrary, a public figure such as Anne Frank, is "approachable" and there is a reason she is almost immediately the access point for young children's connection to the Holocaust. "It is an empathetic way to touch on a scary subject and to start talking." However, the threat of dilution lingers, and the farther away—and abstracted—the Holocaust becomes for the younger generation, the greater this threat of dilution is. Similarly, The International March of the Living, an annual education program that brings individuals from all over the world to Poland and Israel "in order to study the history of the Holocaust and to examine the roots of prejudice, intolerance and hate" is both applauded and criticized. There is no need to deny or question the impact this journey has on those already connection to the Holocaust (especially as the trips are often accompanied or lead by survivors). The March of the Living is a root of education, a way to engage the disengaged, whereby conversations can be had and serious questions can then be considered. The real root of disengagement stems from the current generation. Whereas it was often taken as a given by the second generation that they lived with the horrors of the Holocaust (in a large number of ways), the grandchildren of survivors often find themselves possessing a strong sense of urgency to tell over stories, hear from survivors and educate themselves in order to continue the transmission of both history and memory. However, the danger lies in the current generation, where there two routes are found. The first is to completely do everything in one's power to make sure these stories get passed on and Holocaust education continues. But, there are also those who are not interested—perhaps because it was an event of the past, perhaps because they have no connection, or perhaps because they see other atrocities currently going on in the world around them and are focusing on the present. The first and second generations have their own respective distinctions, but the third generation is where it gets tricky—they are both abstracted and diluted in grappling with the Holocaust.

The next generation is awakened by personal stories and unique forms of engagement, like technology and the visual. It is not enough for them to read about atrocities in historical form. Textbook studies in school curricula provide a framework and basic contextual history, but, for the most part, do not spark engagement and discussion. The Holocaust needs to be taught with methods that are unconventional, because it is an unconventional subject. Sara J. Bloomfield, Director of the USHMM in Washington, D.C. has said that "more than 500,000 students visit the museum annually, but 'attracting and sustaining their attention is an increasing challenge.' The museum has increased its emphasis on personal stories and ideas — in addition to facts and events — in hopes of drawing in young people. Technology was important too, given its popularity with young people, 'but it must be effective in generating engagement and learning,' Ms. Bloomfield said." Museums are also fighting Holocaust deniers and revisionists-- an even greater risk as survivors are dying out and firsthand accounts of the Holocaust are fading. "There is no question that dilution is a fear, but the chance to express the experience is much greater because we have these concrete places that people can go to", explains Steven Ludsin, son of survivors and member of the first Holocaust Commission. Are these places enough, especially for the third generation?

The Transmission of Memory

Regarding intergenerational transmission, it is oral history that in essence, authorizes the transmission of memory. For a memory to form there is an element of permission we give our brain to allow space for more to form. A memory is typically accessible (at least in some sort of way) -- for the simple reason that if it weren't, it would not exist. The more we engage with this idea, the more the memory itself forms, and, as it does, continues to occupy space in our brains; and, the more we tell over recollections, the more we keep spinning this web of oral history. Oral history is complex as its essence lies on trust. Trust on the part of the narrator, to tell over the story, to provide accurate details, to tell those who will continue to give over these accounts, and to rely on their own formed memory. On the other hand, the receiver exhibits an element of trust as he/she choses to take in the account and, in a sense, take ownership. As Hirsch explains, the memory "once spoken" takes on new meaning; to keep telling over a spoken account is like a game of telephone—words get lost in the transmission, sentences blur and new ideas emerge. While this shift occurs when the spoken is past down, from the lips of one to the ears of the next, memory itself undergoes a parallel change. Whether the recollection passes from one physical realm to another, or just from one individual's mental context to another, it gets molded and shaped according to a number of factors. Every individual, and every generation, engages with this act of transmission differently.

Memory is, for the most part, preserved by engagement. Forms of engagement include speaking, writing, creative arts and allowing the memory to be transmitted. However, this is increasingly difficult in the case of traumatic remembrances, particularly those with such strong, tangible elements. How do places play a role in memory? Landscape is one trigger of memory; it simultaneously releases and creates impressions. Traumatic memories can be turned on in less than a second when an individual connects to a specific place of recognition. How do spaces of the past stay with us as we venture into tomorrow? Time and space lend way to memory and consciousness, and landscapes appear to possess the power to both erase and commemorate genocide. In his *Landscapes of Holocaust Postmemory,* Brett Kaplan seeks to investigate how the Holocaust travels through contemporary geographies. Not only does the

Holocaust travel through geographies via memory or physical spaces where memory was formed, but it is also this very notion that brings museums to the stage. Museums-- specific sites of engagement-- often serve as landscapes of Holocaust postmemory, specifically for the later generations. Holocaust museums precisely seem to work like this; that is, they create these images and ideas of that time in history, and this memory becomes the memory of the visitor. Then, as we often automatically do, we begin to associate certain locales with ideas and emotions, forming a wholly comprehensive psychological experience. Museums themselves are sites of pilgrimage, of preservation, of archives, of research, and, of memory. To engage with these sites is to generate memory in a unique way. As survivors are dying out, the burden of testimony falls to subsequent generations, and perhaps even to landscapes and memorial structures to bear permanence. Postmemory— "a consequence of traumatic recall but at a generational remove" -- plays a role in this, as it seems that the physical sites themselves are generating memories and stories which have been given over to researchers and historians.

But, does a physical place align more with the idea of change and ephemerality, or with perpetuity? Kaplan explains that these landscapes of horror "can bear only unstable witness." Whether this is a physical landscape or a psychological one, "the dynamic tension between memory and forgetting appears... as it traces divergent iterations of our relationship to the past." Kaplan uses the term landscape to refer to imaginative and literary landscapes as well as "the concrete existence of spaces where events associated with the Nazi regime and its atrocities happened forces us to grapple with how time affects trauma, with how memory embeds in space." While Kaplan appears to be referring to first-hand memory, I am looking to later accounts, namely third-hand accounts qua postmemory. Herein lies an inherent contradiction that throws a wrench into the whole notion of memory with regard to trauma. It is known that trauma affects memory in a number of ways. The descendants of victim survivors, as well as of perpetrators and bystanders who witnessed these harrowing events connect so deeply to the previous generations' remembrances that they render that connection a form of memory. Hirsch posits that in certain "extreme circumstances, memory can be transferred to those who were not actually there to live an event." As is the case of physical places, the idea of "post" occupies "an uneasy oscillation between continuity and rupture," toying the line between truthful recall and a scarred imagination. Now, to not only examine the second-degree of postmemory, but to analyze how museums and memorials carry already transferred memory, is a conduit for which to evaluate where and how the idea of genocide today, in 2017, is presented.

Foundations of History and Memory

A sort of historical deja-vu, postmemory is a second order, a proxy for memory. So too, museum spaces—particularly Holocaust museums—are a form of space where memory exists. Therefore, we can conceptualize Holocaust museums as a technology for this notion of postmemory mediated by space. Do museums operate as apparatuses of memory a result of the space itself, or as a result of what's within the space? How do survivors of the Holocaust utilize these institutions? If we are to say that museums are a proxy for postmemory, they are, in a sense, a "substitute survivor generation" for those with no [generational] connection to the Holocaust. Moreover, one who lived through this time doesn't need a museum if museums serve as memory itself—they already have their own memories. Today, museums have more power than ever. As the number of living survivors continues to diminish, we, as the next generations, have a burden of responsibility to carry on their legacy and to expose the world to the true facts surrounding this time. With those carrying the first order of memory gone, museums come to the forefront, stepping in as an order of memory—particularly a wholly encapsulating postmemory. Built for those whose memory of the Holocaust will be a postmemory, the museum is a medium that triggers active imaginations. However, there is risk in this, as Kaplan explains, "sometimes monumental structures erase rather than commemorate."

When we think about museums, we think about representation and space. Holocaust museums, particularly, are sites that toy the line between factual history and artifacts and memory and emotion; one might even deploy this tension as one of logos versus pathos. Not only does the notion of space bring forth the dichotomy between reclamation, moving on, and memorialization, holding on, but it also treads with the difference between history and memory. Whereas history deals with hard facts and the particulars of what happened, memory is filed with perspective and emotion. Identification is another notion particularly aligned with memory. Aptly put by Lee Klein, "memory is not a property of individual minds, but a diverse and shifting collection of material artifacts and social practices." To deal with history is to deal with facts on a page—a one dimensional archive; to deal with memory is a whole other question—it is (more than) three dimensional, filling up space in the brain with all kinds of perspectives, oralities and recollections. Whereas history is *your* story, memory is, in a sense, *my* story. An identity creator and tool of deception, memory is malleable and conductible, like a piece of metal, but, it is also fragile and can easily be manipulated— it is "the most fragile and capricious of our faculties." And, whereas history is transmitted by chronicle, memory is transmitted by ritual and recital. What is remembered is not always recorded, and vice versa. In the context of the Holocaust, this serves as a double-edged sword. For Herodotus— "the Father of History" — "the writing of history was first and foremost a bulwark against the inexorable erosion of memory endangered by the passage of time." To write history is to assign it permanence but it also simultaneously renders it fleeting, as memory has the potential to be become fuzzy and diluted. But memory is strong. It elicits the feeling of custodianship for the memory-bearer, and it provides "a living link between generations," as Halwach states. It is hard to get rid of, even if that link seems a bit dormant at times. Ever successfully shaken a traumatic memory from your mind? Thoughts still linger there, albeit inactively. On the flip side, a positive memory is something we often want to refer to, but cannot always fully activate, especially as we move forward in time. Halbrach's *La Memoire Collective* and Yerushalmi's *Zakhor* (which grasps its basic framework in place from Halbrach), contend that "there exists an unbridgeable gap between historiography and memory." To them, collective memory belongs to pre-modern societies that were rooted in tradition and social practices, whereas the discipline of history came about later, to a more modern society in the nineteenth century. Yet now, especially in the context of Holocaust studies and commemoration, this does not seem to be the case. Memory provides history to us today, especially by way of first-hand accounts. "History is kept alive through preserving historical sources of all kinds--documents, oral testimony, memoirs, artifacts. It is also preserved through analysis of those sources in monographs and synthetic works--through writing good history. To rely on memory alone is a mistake," Professor Richard Breitman explains. "Memories change with the passage of time, which is why scholars have to treat them carefully, with respect." While we have the history of WWII written down, it is the reports and recollections of those who lived through it who provide us with the whole picture— we need both.

In the Jewish tradition, we have the written Torah and the oral Torah, both immensely sacred. Written history has the potential to be physically lost, while oral history has the potential to be lost in translation. Yosef Haim Yerushalmi's classic text, *Zakhor,* weaves through Jewish history and Jewish memory, exploring the tension between the two while stressing the importance of harnessing both history and memory. "The choice of Jews (and non-Jews) is not whether or not to have a past, but rather—what kind of past shall we have." And, not only what kind of past we shall have, but where that past lays. Is it carried on? Through what means? How influential is that past for the future? Bringing the aforementioned to the context of the Holocaust, we can begin to discern where memory is situated. A simple statement, "The Holocaust is one of the best documented atrocities in history," by Yehuda Bauer bears so much weight. We have the historical records, the photographs, the numbers, and the architectural evidence (a whole other argument on Holocaust denial lays here). It is memory, however, that brings layers upon layers of background and meaning to these tangible artifacts. For a Holocaust survivor to give over her memory, her testimony, is to relay much more than memory. We need these testimonies. Now, more than ever, memory is in the process of being diluted as generations pass, posing potential danger of treating the Holocaust as a distant horror. To preserve these testimonies and experiences is not only (first and foremost) a respect to the survivors, but an obligation for the coming generations.

Frederick Nietzsche's "On the Advantages and Disadvantages of History" is perhaps, where the notion of *using* history for life emerges. "Historical education is wholesome and promising for the future only in the service of a powerful new life-giving influence", whereby he is asserting that this is the only purpose for which history should be employed. "The capacity to build a new future," he demands, "depends on our ability to see a fundamental continuity with the strengths of the past." History is not an end in itself, but rather a means to serving life. Nietzsche, however, does not imply that this is always the case—he also emphasizes "the capacity to live *unhistorically*", or with the ability to forget. The real way to move forward is to recognize when to live historically—using history for life—and when to live unhistorically. Using the history of WWII and the Holocaust actively—*for life*—has the potential to truly be beneficial in our everyday understanding of the times we live in, as well as the future. Yet, Nietzsche's idea of the function of history is further deepened with his three approaches to kinds of history—monumental, antiquarian and critical. In his final approach to history, the critical, Nietzsche explains that in this view "[man] must have the strength... to shatter and dissolve something to enable him to live; this he achieves by dragging it to the bar of judgement, interrogating it meticulously and finally condemning it." This close analysis of history is complicated, and seems contradictory towards his idea of utilizing history, using it as a vehicle through which to move forward. Critical history gives man the ability to condemn that which conflicts with his views which he discovers through this analytical approach, and to "implant a new habit... a second nature so that the first nature withers away." The proper usage of history according to Nietzsche, requires the correct usage of the three views of history. Critical history is essential subsequent to the other two (monumental, antiquarian) as it allows man to move forward for growth and progress.

Generations of Postmemory

In navigating the shift away from historical facts and records and over to the realm of memory, how do we remember and make sense of these facts today, generations later? Perhaps one of the most difficult struggle with memory is dealing with the accounts of the perpetrators, and the generations that succeed them. Out of this came measures of transitional justice like the Nuremberg Trials, but also raised questions about collective memory and guilt. Can a nation as a whole be held responsible for crimes? Legal scholar Martha Minow has explored some of the dilemmas of transitional justice. She writes:

> "Societies have to struggle over how much to acknowledge, whether to punish, and how to recover. How to treat the continuing presence of perpetrators, and victims, and bystanders, after the violence has ended is a central problem, or better put, series of problems. A common formulation posits the two dangers of wallowing in the past and forgetting it. Too much memory or not enough; too much enshrinement of victimhood or insufficient memorializing of victims and

survivors; too much past or too little acknowledgement of the past's staging of the present; these joined dangers accompany not just societies emerging from mass violence, but also individuals recovering from trauma."

In the years following the Holocaust, Germany has faced these questions and enacted a number of measures in an attempt to reconcile with them. The number of second generation Germans came to terms with their lineage and were willing to face the past and condemn the actions of their parents. But with these measures of transitional justice came complex debates regarding the testimony of the tried perpetrators. Where does their memory lay? Could the testimonies they give over bear weight; could we use the memory of these monsters, or is nothing related to them trustworthy or legitimate? Take, for instance, Nazi war criminal Adolf Eichmann's 1960 trial in Jerusalem, particularly as reported on by Hannah Arendt, a European escapee and noted writer. What was remarkable about Eichmann's trial was the concept coined by Arendt of "the banality of evil" whereas Eichmann was not seen as a full-blown monster, but rather came into this evil as a result of thoughtlessness and conformation. The trial featured Eichmann behind bulletproof glass, owning a blasé attitude and putting up an evasive front. Arendt, as reporting on the way Eichmann carried himself and testified throughout the trial, at one point in her report notes that "Eichmann needed only to recall the past in order to feel sure he was not lying." () Is this testimony to be trusted? While one can argue that we (or mostly, we) wanted to hear this monster plead guilty and take responsibility for his implementation of the Final Solution (although, according to Gerald Rettinger it was Heydrich who was "the real engineer of the Final Solution), to what extent to we take Eichmann's testimony at face value? Arendt continues in her report to relay that "Eichmann's mind was filled…his memory proved to be very unreliable."

How do third generation survivors react to this trial? To Arendt's thesis that Eichmann was not born a monster, but was an ordinary human reduced to an individual who followed orders? And, how do third generation survivors of perpetrators and bystanders react to the Holocaust as whole? Rudolf Hoss, founder and first commandant of Auschwitz-Birkenau concentration camp is another fascinating subject to study in light of the transmission of memory. A mastermind of mass extermination and a participant in the greatest crime in history, Hoss was executed in 1947 for his role in perpetrating Crimes Against Humanity. While awaiting his death sentence, Hoss wrote his autobiography—an account of his memories of the life he lived. In it, he explains how he buried himself in work, resulting in his becoming "unapproachable and visibly hardened," similar to the way Arendt postulates that Eichmann morphed into a perpetrator of genocide. Hoss, like other human beings, had descendants. His grandson, Rainer Hoss, discovered his legacy at the ripe age of 12, when he was beaten by a gardener at his boarding school after learning he was the grandson of the monster Rudolph Hoss. Rainer Hoss describes that brutal experience with intense recall: "He beat me, because he projected on me all the horror he went through... Once a Hoss, always Hoss. Whether you are the grandfather of the grandson- guilty is guilty." What is interesting about the perpetrators in regard to the notion of postmemory and museums is that they are sometimes showcased and given a place there. Yad Vashem, for example, has plaques of top SS commanders. There was a great deal of debate surrounding this idea when the museum first opened. Why give them a place and memory? Furthermore, why here, right alongside the victims and survivors? How much power does memory and place hold?

On this wall of Yad Vashem sits a black and white portrait of Rudolf Hoss, with a small plaque describing who he was, what he was instrumental in, and where. Not only is Rainer Hoss haunted by the information he continues to learn about the Holocaust and his grandfather, but the he also recalls the cold nature of his father—the result of the connection between the prior generation of Rudolph and Hans-Jurgen (his father)— and the tough household he grew up. Not too long ago, Rainer Hoss ventured to Auschwitz with a friend and a third-generation survivor. During this trip, he met a group of young Israeli students, descendants of survivors, to whom he explained the purpose of his trip— "to see the horror my grandfather made and all the lies the family made." An intense and emotional few days for Hoss brought him to an important realization that was somewhat comforting for him—he realized that third generation Jews did not hold him accountable for his grandfather's acts of monstrosity. To engage with the recollection of the minds of evil is one thing, however to explore the post memory of subsequent generations of these masterminds is another. Does this idea of post memory apply to them? To what extent do the children and grandchildren of Eichmann and Hoss seek to explore the testimonies of their respective grandfathers—do they draw upon them, either to express remorse or pride, or do they seek to push them away, to throw them into the ocean with the ashes of their grandfathers? Moreover, to contrast the subsequent generations of survivors of the Holocaust with the decedents of the perpetrators would be (in my opinion), disrespectful and utterly wrong. However, to engage with the notion of memory and to explore the phenomenon of transmission, looking at the two may provide for an extremely nuanced analysis of the way different second and third generations interact with memory.

Aptly put by the historian Marcus Lee Hansen, "What the son wishes to forget the grandson wishes to remember." For years, the second generation of Holocaust survivors have been studied and analyzed. This is an extremely complex group to study, and an even more complicated one to generalize. Every second generation's situation is different as a result of a number of factors: What kind of experience did their parents have? How did their parents try to cope in the postwar years? Did their parents speak openly about the Holocaust? Or, did they never even so utter a word? The list goes on and on, as does the analysis. And, moreover, while some children became obsessed with the Holocaust, others found themselves on the complete opposite side of the spectrum. Sometimes a certain amount of time was needed to pass with distance in order to approach this scarring matter objectively. "The second generation lapsed into silence because it took cues from the first generation," explains sociologist and historian William Helmreich. Trajectories of memory encounter a blockage here, and it is at this very place in time that postmemory comes to the stage; one might even argue that postmemory begins to dominate the notion of remembrance during this generational break. Dr. Ruth Beckerman, in her *Die papierene brucke*, asks "who are we, children of the second generation? What characterizes us? How can one gain access to the childhood of one's parents?" The urgency, this crisis of knowledge surrounding the hazy, horrid years of WWII become even more complicated when memory comes into play. Another common approach for the second generation was to accept the fact that their childhood would be unusual, and they often took this as a given. The groundbreaking research into "Transgenerational Effects" examines this so called "survivor syndrome" and the object relations theory—the theory that human motivation comes from people's need to relate to others. Here, it is linked to the relationship with parent. "The children of survivors show symptoms which would be expected if they actually lived through the Holocaust... they seem to share an anguished collective memory of the Holocaust in both their dreams and fantasies reflective of recurrent references to their parents' traumatic experiences." Dr. Helmreich's noted book, "Against All Odds: Holocaust Survivors and the Successful Lives They Made in America," looks at this notion of "survivor syndrome." Does it persist? One might one wonder-- does it inherently lie within DNA? Helmreich, however, flips this premise on its head, instead studying the traits of those that survived. His late 20th century study's results brought the successful lives of Holocaust survivors to light, rather than the previously studied troubled survivors. Along with this study comes the question of the second generation, not yet fully formulated at the time of Dr. Helmreich's scientific research endeavor. When asked about the second generation and the transmission of memory, Dr. Helmreich convened the discussion by framing it as wholly circumstantial. Many survivors say they survived through "luck," He then immediately turned to a discussion he had with Eli Wiesel, who, when he told him he felt survivors had certain traits and skills, responded "it was just luck." Second generation children of survivors are perhaps the most complex generation to study. A great deal spent their lives worrying, analyzing, wondering what their parents had to do to survive. While the first generation—the survivors themselves—carried survivor guilt, many of their children held onto this as well, for a number of reasons. "The second generation lapsed into silence because they took cues from the first generation," explains Helmreich. Like Eliezer Berkovitz asserted in his "Faith After the Holocaust," we can't say because we weren't there, we cannot judge or even attempt to begin to fathom life during that time. So too, the subsequent generations. Moreover, it seems that the third and fourth generations can't even look to the second generation like this. Just as we cannot begin to understand living during the time of the Holocaust, so too, we, as later generations, cannot look at those who grew up as the children of survivors and the psychological effects of their lives.

Intergenerational transmission in children of survivors who were not directly exposed to the same trauma as their parents are the result of both relational and biological processes, as is often carried on for generations. Dr. Irit Felsen, explains that "despite attempts to defend against it, adult-onset trauma pervades every self-state and manifests in daily life in a spectrum of phenomena, ranging from symptoms and fragments of intrusive experiences, through various degrees of enactments in relationships, in social and political attitudes, and in pervasive life themes." Furthermore, the trauma-related symptoms and traumatic recall in a survivor parent "permeates the relational intersubjective field and might lead the trauma survivor's child to perceive the parent as fearful or frightening." Posttraumatic symptoms can persist for decades, as evident by was of the largest body of intergenerational transmission studies, in the children of Holocaust survivors. What was observed in these studies were themes of relational experiences, whereby the children of survivors suffered from numbing and detachment during certain joyous life occasions and various manifestations of parental inability to provide care, emotional support and communicate effectively with their children. "The impact of directly experiencing parental intrusive memories and parental distress" was also a key observation. Here, we see the way postmemory and psychology amalgamate. Felsen further proclaims that "in order to meet the needs of current trauma survivors, it is important to resist social and professional tendencies to deny the impact of adult-onset trauma." Immediately following the war, survivors were often met with facials of denial and accusations. This was a time of denial and neglect, and a time when survivors need help the most. Often alienated from "normal"— for those who had not experienced trauma, there was a lack of resources, safe spaces and "'a relational home' in which the reverberations of trauma can be expressed and shared." "Lacking an intersubjective context within which they could be voiced, my feelings of sorrow and horror lived largely in my body, devolving into vegetative states of exhaustion and lethargy," explains Stolorow. Therefore, most trauma had no outlet, and survivors carried this with them, and, in turn, this transmission manifested itself through generations in a myriad of ways (perhaps providing reason for the incredible number of coping mechanisms we have seen from Holocaust survivors and their children). Today, contemporary psychoanalytic thinking about adult-onsent trauma "integrates diverse perspectives and even conflicting 'truths' about the complexities of trauma and recovery." This is an important understanding and can be applied in the case of "historical trauma." It also requires that "we confront 'our own never finished business of avoiding denial while living in an age of genocide and under the aura of uncontained destructiveness.' The availability of appropriate treatment for current and future trauma survivors depends on learning from past failures in order to avoid the repeated tendency, reflected in past and present formulations, to deny the reality of traumatic catastrophes." Museums like the USHMM and Yad Vashem take on these roles in different capacities and for different audiences.

For both the United States Holocaust Memorial Museum and Yad Vashem, the physical location aligns with the specific aim of the museum. The former, located among our national monuments to freedom on the National Mall, the Museum provides a powerful lesson in the fragility of freedom, the myth of progress, and the need for vigilance in preserving democratic values. With unique power and authenticity, the Museum teaches millions of people each year about the dangers of unchecked hatred and the need to prevent genocide. And we encourage them to act, cultivating a sense of moral responsibility among our citizens so that they will respond to the monumental challenges that confront our world." It touches on politics, history, current events and moral responsibility. Yad Vashem, on the other hand, seeks to provide the facts to relay the history of the Holocaust. "Both multidisciplinary and interdisciplinary, it presents the story of the Shoah from a unique Jewish perspective, emphasizing the experiences of the individual victims through original artifacts, survivor testimonies and personal possessions." At the end of the Museum's historical narrative(s) is the Hall of Names, a rotunda that houses a repository for the Pages of Testimony from the millions of Holocaust victims who perished. Following this, the visitor continues on to the epilogue and exits to the balcony, opening up to a panoramic view of Jerusalem, the homeland of the Jewish people. The story ends there, and the space leaves the visitor lingering in the gardens and memorials surrounding the History Museum. In contrast, the USHMM exhibit culminates, and the viewer finds themselves in the main hall, with other exhibits to choose from. While Yad Vashem serves its specific audience with the historical narrative, the USHMM presents the

Holocaust to its audience in order to create a lens for which to look at other genocides—two completely separate audiences, intentions and approaches.

Sites as Apparatuses of Postmemory

For a third-generation millennial, going to a Holocaust museum can be a harrowing experience. Museums can also take on forms of postmemory for these visitors, especially if it is their first or only tangible connection to the Shoah. For many young adults, the Holocaust is a distant horror they may or may not have read about in textbooks growing up. But, do museums today have an underlying mission of advocacy, or do they solely provide the evidence for the visitor? How is the mission of Holocaust studies reconfigured in contemporary museums? Do we really use memorialization for the sake of the present, or do we hope to? How is history being used, rather than just known, in order to understand and approach today?

Museums try to present a fuller picture of that era, often starting with life before the Holocaust, during, and many times even, (an attempt at) life after the Holocaust. We often can't comprehend the enormity of what was lost, until we see what was had prior. With the end of the war came the impulse to commemorate the victims of Nazi genocide, and also to honor the heroes, resistance fighters, survivors and righteous among the nations. Initially, these efforts came directly from the survivors themselves, who, erected monuments, wrote memoirs, provided testimony and sought (albeit, minimal) justice. "The sense of urgency to mark the Holocaust increased as the actual events grew ever more distant and as the survivors aged, "and in subsequent decades, museums and monuments began to rise throughout the globe. What is interesting here is the timing. The earliest Holocaust museums and memorials emerged when there was only the first generation of survivors. The first Holocaust memorial was established by a group of courageous survivors themselves, who took ashes from the crematoriums, desecrated Torah scrolls and small objects that they survived with in the camps. The Chamber of the Holocaust, tucked away in a cave-like maze of rooms in the Old City of Jerusalem started off as a memorial, but soon became a raw and astonishingly jarring museum with minimal curation. Each dark and damp cave is covered with memorial plaques of towns that were destroyed; there are thousands of them, wall to wall in these cramped quarters. Nothing here is abstracted or diluted. An album of photographs lays dormant on an old wooden table, a note taped to it "viewer discretion is highly advised." Black and white photographs of humiliated Jews in Poland are propped against the stone walls, the same walls that used to surround the holiest place in the world for the Jews, the Temple. In another room, three bars of soap are in wooden and glass chest, with a simple engraved message explaining that the soap was apparently made from the fat of the Jews who were murdered in the camps. The center room, the biggest and most open—but still incredibly eerie, damp and dark-- bears a large grave for all the unknown murdered, and for (the almost all) who were not buried properly. Six wreaths are placed on top, and six canisters with ashes from six concentration camps. The survivors did not enlist curators, architects and psychologists for this memorial—they simply needed a space to memorialize when they got to Israel three years later. The artifacts and visitors who came in the following years helped change the Chamber of the Holocaust to a museum as well as a memorial, a museum that showed the true horrors of the Holocaust in a totally shocking and raw way. It is a place of the past, of memorialization and remembrance, but not particularly one of education. It is often overlooked, significantly underfunded (it survives on donations) and wholly undiluted.

The opening of the United States Holocaust Museum became the epicenter for Holocaust commemoration in the United States, and the early 21st century saw an increase in the amount of research and scholarly work devoted to the era of the Holocaust. It was created as a place to examine what happened, how it happened, and *if it could happen again*. The United States' official memorial, the United States Holocaust Memorial Museum, was erected next to the National Mall in Washington, D.C. on April 22, 1993. When the plans started for the museum towards the end of the 20th century, President Jimmy Carter established the President's Commission on the Holocaust on November 1, 1978, chaired by Elie Wiesel, prominent author and Holocaust survivor. The main mandate of this commission was to investigate the creation and maintenance of a memorial to victims of the Holocaust. This then morphed in the U.S. Holocaust Memorial Council. Members of the delegation traveled to other countries, museums and memorials to receive artifacts and develop a deeper understanding how the different Holocaust memorials and museums serve different geographic locations and peoples. Jeshajahu Weinberg, the first director of the museum summed up his mission in the first Museum newsletter in 1993. "I don't want people to come out of the museum with conclusions. I want them to come out with impression. If this museum can bring you to the point where you begin thinking about what you've seen and applying it somehow to your world, then we will have succeeded." The museum was not meant to elicit a response, rather "it is a question mark. If there is a response, it is a response in responsibility." Elie Wiesel, in his speech at the dedication of the United States Holocaust Museum on Thursday, April 22, 1993 most notably stated "for the dead and the living, we must bear witness." This is engraved in stone at the entrance of the museum, as he explained "not only are we responsible for the memories of the dead, we are also responsible for what we are doing with those memories." This, perhaps, set the tone of this endeavor, and a created a footing for which to establish the mission and specific objectives of the space itself.

The architect James Freed was tasked with the formidable challenge of creating a space of both remembrance and education, a combination of the past, the present and the future. Upon the appointment of Freed, Elie Wiesel said, "the Holocaust in its enormity defies language and art, and yet both must be used to tell the tale, the tale that must be told." Central debates about the philosophy behind having a space, and about the space itself, arose from the need to understand how to present the Holocaust to the public, but also to those immediately affected by it. To make the space functionally viable, Freed had to lessen the intensity of his original design, however, to dilute it too much would destroy the integrity of the building. "I can't tolerate prettification- that's what the Germans did at the camps with Tyrolean facades and flower-pots on the sills..." he explained in his analyses. The museum made a shattering impact on the American public, as it proved that "civilized architecture can deal with the uncivilized." In 1993, Herbert Muschamp previewed the museum. To him, the building "invites interpretation but confounds analysis. Its monumental forms appear to be shaped not by architecture but by history. It is not a building about the past. It is about the historical present. Is compels us to see that events transpired half a century ago have not lost their grip on the world." This same statement could be written today, in 2017. Currently, the museum showcases "Cambodia 1975-1979", an exhibit on Cambodia's Khmer Rouge genocide which took place years after the Holocaust. On the lower level of the museum, perpendicular to this exhibition is one titled "A Dangerous Life: The Protocols of the Elders of Zion" which explored the continuing impact of the most widely distributed anti-Semitic publication of modern times. This was also one of the key anti-Semitic texts that the Nazi's used. Unfortunately, the historical present that Muschamp sees the museum manifesting is not one in which we have learned from the Holocaust, rather it is one in which we continuously see history rhyming.

In a sense, the museum fails to fully implement of the mission of remembrance and education. While it is great that the museum showcases, educates and actively fights past and current injustices, we should not have to be doing this eighty plus years after the Holocaust. Four years before the building was completed, George F. Will wrote in the Washington Post that "it has been said that we make our buildings and then they make us. The museum will make memories for rising generations, expanding their consciousness of the awful possibilities of human action." Yes, the museum fulfills this first part. It provides a postmemorial experience, especially for the third generation and for those otherwise unconnected. But, he continues, "Thus it will be, fundamentally, a museum serving philosophy. It will start from extreme particularity—shoes, bricks, canisters—and an event: Hitler's war against the Jews. However, it will stir visitors to the most general reflections on the nature of humankind (hence the museum's proper place on the Mall) the great questions of governance." We are still struggling with this today. And, while we should constantly be grappling with the nature of mankind—questions of power, collaboration, reach—they should be "the great questions of governance" as we learn from the past and move forward, exploring the depth of mankind, and how much he can accomplish for the good.

Yad Vashem, The World Holocaust Remembrance Center, is Israel's Official Memorial to the Victims of the Holocaust. Originally opened in 1957 as just a building with a library and archives, it has evolved in a cutting-edge memorial museum designed by Moshe Safdie surrounded monuments and trees of remembrance and the largest library of Holocaust information, all set in the hills of Jerusalem. While the USHMM had underlying hints of governance in both its locale and mission, Yad Vashem carries the history of Israel in its location adjacent to Mount Herzl (Israel's national cemetery) and the founding of the state for the Jewish people in the aftermath of the Holocaust. The most common theme surrounding the establishment of the museum, and the redesigning or the new museum in 2005, is "to help shape memory as the 21st century approaches." The museum struggles with the telling of memory in keeping with the tradition, without dulling or diluting memory. Revisionism, and "the battle over memory" reinforces the goals of the museum, as there is a string emphasis on educational and technological capabilities. The museum's chief population was defined as "young Jews belonging to the 3rd and 4th generation, with no personal recollections of the second World War period and the Holocaust." This appears to be the true difference in Yad Vashem's approach—the museum is dedicated to education, and especially dealing with the minds of the young. Whereas the USHMM lens seems to be aimed for the present, Yad Vashem tries to educate the young minds of the past, leaving it up to them to decide how to view today and tomorrow. It is presenting the information, a historical education with a specific reach. "the most important goal of the museum is to make people think. Our museum does not attempt to prescribe specific lessons to be learned" is a goal explicitly outlined in the New Historical Museum. The original museum was staunchly archival and historical—many documents and photographs were exhibited in grayscale alongside a memorial pillar. With time came changes, and the museum felt the need to keep up with the times and the urge to find ways to relate to the audience. From the communication revolution emerged new goals and even a new audience; 1994 posed different questions than 1972. The old museum was established by the survivors of the second World War generation, while the new museum was built by a new generation of Israeli Jews.

From the minute visitors step into the triangular structure built into the hills of Jerusalem, they are streamed into a zig-zagging path—there is no escaping. This is eerily reminiscent of the Holocaust, the winding, suddenly jarring, road of the unknown. It is also representative of the complicated path memory takes, especially as the years pass. The glass roof at the structure lets in small glimmers of sunlight, but it barely bounces around the prismic structure, reminiscent of the righteous among the nations, who shone so bright in their heroic efforts. The new museum, designed by Moshe Safdie and Safdie Architects and curated by Avner Shalev, employs two main modes of representation: one that is special and aesthetic, and the other a representation of narrative and documentation. It also leads the visitor through a path of three narratives—a contextual narrative, a general narrative and an individual narrative—which allows the visitor to choose their story path, but not their physical route. "If the curatorial mission of Yad Vashem is to name the names of those who perished in the Holocaust, even as it is the fate of so many to remain nameless, then the architectural mission is to establish a place, however paradoxically, it is to be a place of displacement." The space itself folds into the curated memory; it serves as a shell. Whereas memory is a shell that was once a body--"a disembodied thought or reflection" --architecture is shell that is "a form of embodiment." The museum oscillates between the two; it is simultaneously enclosing and claustrophobic, but also exhibits vastness and infinite continuity.

While the USHMM seeks to educate viewers to act, and Yad Vashem aims to provide the historical facts of the Holocaust, the Museum of Jewish Heritage in Battery Park, New York City, houses "a Living Memorial to the Holocaust." This Living Memorial, a pyramid structure that tops the building, finds itself across from the Statue of Liberty and Ellis Island. This roof is reminiscent of the six million Jews who perished, and of the six-pointed Jewish star, emphasizing the museum's commitment to "representing Jewish life and cultures as it has endured and evolved." The Museum of Jewish Heritage – A Living Memorial to the Holocaust is "New York's contribution to the global responsibility to never forget. The Museum is committed to the crucial mission of educating diverse visitors about Jewish life before, during, and after the Holocaust." Prior to the museum's opening in 1997, there were questions of whether or not we needed another museum dedicated to the Holocaust after the opening of the USHMM in D.C. However, the Museum of Jewish Heritage strongly invests in the life of the Jews before (and after) the Holocaust. This is the fundamental difference between this museum and the other, especially in understanding the way this genocide is seen by the third and fourth generation. Only once you know what was, can you begin to fully comprehend what was lost. Yad Vashem also works with this idea with its video installation, "The Living Landscape", projected upon entry.

These three museums work in tandem, but also in severance. While their mission statements are different, their goals are similar—to educate. Museums use memorialization for the sake of the present, and this is exceptionally evident in the approaches of all three. Today, museums have more power than ever as they can trigger memories—whether postmemory or an authentic memory—and serve as a critical lens for understanding how to *use* history, rather than just *knowing* it. While some museums have an active mission in the realm of advocacy, others take a more passive approach in providing historical context and evidence for the reader to become active. While widely debated, critiqued, praised and condemned, the aforementioned approaches—museums, heritage trips, textbook education, oral testimonies-- are all a start. The role of sites of commemoration and memorialization have changed with the passing of time and the dwindling of the Holocaust survivors. What will happen when the last survivor is no more? We don't know. We are charged with the task of grappling with this phenomenon, and continuing to work with the implications of a cultural consciousness of heightened passing. The third generation that finds itself both abstracted and diluted, shielded and linked, needs to continue to find ways to actively engage in education and discussion, because this is how we can use history to serve the present. This is also how we can fill the links between generations and carry on the stories of survivors and those who perished. We owe it to them.

Postscript

In August of 2017, almost a year after my first visit to my Holocaust survivor in Brooklyn, I found myself walking up the connecting path between Yad Vashem and Mount Herzl in the blazing heat of midday Jerusalem, tears streaming down my face. Tears of awe and of acclaim, for a nation rebuilt and a land flowing with milk and honey, strength and innovation. But also tears of admiration and of wonder, for the righteous among the nation, still fighting for tolerance and standing up to hatred today. And tears of sorrow and of memorialization, for those who perished in the face of evil, who never got to see this dream. But as I ventured down further, and made my way down the stone steps and security gate and over to the Archives and Library Building for my closing day of research, I realized that these were mainly tears of distress. For after decades of hatred, intolerance and mass atrocities, evil is still on the rise, veering its ugly head in new forms, but also in those tried and true.

Later that day, after hours in the Yad Vashem archives, looking at press releases and plans surrounding the new Historical

Museum (unveiled in 2005), and talking to strangers from around the world working in the library, I found glimmers of strength in knowing what lengths people—of all ages, religions, nationalities, occupations and beliefs- go to in order to continue to educate and to memorialize. While I originally sought out to "understand genocide", these nine months taught me precisely the opposite— there is no way to understand genocide. From the onset of this endeavor I saw that there was no way to answer my research question, but I thought I may find a few similar approaches. Rather, I ended up learning the ways that evil can manifest itself, and how every individual, and generation, reacts to this differently. And as I made my way to my final stop, The Chamber in the Holocaust in the Old City of Jerusalem, I began to realize that while museums carry a huge burden, especially for the third generation, they can share some of it with smaller attestations like conversations, photographs, works of art, physical landscapes and memorials. Standing alone in the dark chamber hidden in the exterior walls of the Old City, I found myself engaging with a new form of postmemory—one that was for me, raw and jarring, neither abstracted or diluted. It was then that I realized how much power these smaller sites, objects and conversations carry, and how, for some, little power museums can carry, as was the case with the schoolchildren from Virginia. If there is one overarching idea I've grappled with over the course of this research, it's the question that asks about the third generation: "How do we, belonging to the generations who did not witness the Holocaust, arrive at an ethical mode of reading in which we do not simply appropriate experiences that we did not live in order to 'extend memory into the present.? "

How do we begin these conversations? How do we approach individuals differently? We desperately need these museums, and we also need these conversations, these photographs and the visual arts. But we also need to learn. Since the end of WWII, we have seen more than forty-three instances of genocide that have caused the death of close to 50 million people. "Never again" we mean, but we are really just repeating "never again?" We are in a vicious cycle of history rhyming throughout the globe. Less than seven days later, back in the United States, I launched the Twitter app on my phone. News of the "Unite the Right" rally which brought hundreds of white supremacists to Charlottesville, Virginia blew up my feed. This rally, on August 12, 2017, could have taken place in 1939

Germany, with hundreds holding torches, flying Nazi flags and chanting "Death to the Jews." Maybe history not only rhymes, but does indeed have the capacity to repeat itself.

Acknowledgments

In July of 2017, at 22 years old, I first started to understand the real meaning of the word "hatred." This was not necessarily on purpose, but the sad reality was that it came about as a result of the times we live in. The 2016 election found itself awash with venomous words, strong statements and harsh realities. It was during that time that I first started to think about the true meaning behind charged words like "evil" "hate" and "destruction." It was also during this time that I became aware of the implications of actions, the very real way that these strong words can manifest themselves, wiping out entire peoples, cultures and areas. As I thought more about this, and about my recent visits with Holocaust survivors, I began to think critically about the word evil itself—is it thrown around too freely today? I wanted to know how both Holocaust survivors and the subsequent generations felt about this word. To me, an ignorant 22-year-old native New Yorker, the Holocaust was a traumatic event of the past, and I genuinely could not (and still cannot) comprehend the enormity of it. I'm not quite sure if it's because of how historically distant it is, or because of the trauma it carries, but in either case, I have been led to think that an atrocity of that caliber could not happen again.

And yet, I am consistently fighting with, and challenging, this notion. How is it that more than seventy years later I turn on my phone and am overtaken with images of Nazi flags, torches and anti-semitic chants just a few states away? Why is there a movement to make the swastika a trendy symbol to wear on a t-shirt? Why are Jews still being kidnapped, tortured, attacked and murdered just for being Jewish? We have seen this all too often; we have been fighting for tolerance since the days of creation. We have seen too many genocides, hate crimes and mass killings since the Holocaust to be able to say "Never Again." Today, in 2017, we are still asking "Never Again?" When will we no longer need to ask this; when will this be a statement, upheld by the people inhabiting this beautiful world we live in, that seems to always be threatened?

I have been thinking about this a lot the past ten months as I took time to shift from my studies and pursue an independent research project, "Understanding Genocide: Inter-generational Abstraction and Dilution through Three Generations Grappling with the Holocaust." I am eternally grateful to all those who opened my eyes during this time, and to those fighting this battle. My inquiry has taken me all over the world, from New York to D.C. to Oxford and to Israel and in contact with individuals around the globe. I thank every single person I've met during these months and I am proud to know that there are so many trying to prove me wrong. As I close this chapter of my research I am curious to see what's to come.

***

My deepest appreciation for a number of individuals and organizations whose guidance, support, input and insight have made this endeavor not only possible, but an incredibly rewarding and humbling experience. To the Gallatin Jewish Studies Grant Committee, thank you for your generous support, and to Professors Stacy Pies and Dr. Eugene Vydrin who believed in this project from its very inception. To Professors Jack Salzman and Dr. Dina Rosenfeld, for planting the seeds of these difficult questions, and for your support and guidance from this project's very inception. To Scott Fisher and Professor Duncombe for their help securing and supervising my CAIHS supervision so that I can conduct interviews. And, to my academic advisors and mentors, Dr. Cyd Cipolla, Emily Stone and Dr. Peter Rajsingh who have, and continue to provide me with, unlimited academic support throughout my academic studies and beyond.

This project took me to places both near and far, whether to visit institutions, museums, specific individuals or conferences. To the incredibly inspirational Cheri Srour in Brooklyn, thank you for sharing your research and opinions with me. To Dr. Irit Felsen and Dr. Eva Fogelman, and to Dr. Yael Granot-Bein, Dr. Carol Kidron and Dr. Nurit Novis at the Weiss-Livnat International Program for Holocaust Studies at Haifa University for your recommendations and references. To Rachelle Goldstein at the ADL/Hidden Child Foundation and Laura Robertson at the International Holocaust Remembrance Alliance and Elizabeth Anthony at the United States Holocaust Memorial, thank you for your time, answers and suggestions. To those I was fortunate enough to interview both virtually and in person: Steven Ludsin, William Helmreich and the Spitz family, as well as numerous Holocaust survivors in the tristate area, as well as my contemporaries who provided their questions and ideas. To Serena Dykman, an incredible inspiration who is working to educate the next generation by sharing her compelling family story. A huge thank you to Professor Richard Breitman, whom I never met in person, but provided insight and answers to interview questions at the initial stages of my project, as well as advice in the final publishing stages. And, to the editors, publishers and scholars who were the first to read this manuscript and guide me from major publishing houses to academic journals and literary magazines—I appreciate your leads and suggestions.

Furthermore, to those who helped me bring this to the present day, and challenge me to see the implications of anti-semitism today. To Dr. Charles Small, who invited me to participate in the 2017 ISGAP-Oxford Summer Institute with the most incredible and inspiring group of researchers in the world— words cannot explain how fortunate I am to have had this experience. To my fellow scholars-in-residence, thank you for showing me what real work is, and what relentless determination can do. You are true righteous gentiles and I am blessed to know you. To the Simon Wiesenthal Center and the Government Advocacy Internship Program, and Michael Cohen and David Blechman at the SWC, thank you for giving me a chance to work on my advocacy skills and learn from true leaders. And to my fellow interns and fellows, thank you for your comradery, support and the stimulating discussions we've had over the course of the fellowship and after. I would be typing all day if I were to list every single person who helped and inspired me this past year, but please know that I have a place in my heart for each and every one of you.

To my parents and sisters, who supported, challenged, raised questions and gave guidance during this unique and unconventional endeavor—thank you from the bottom of my heart. This was an intense subject to immerse myself in, and having you and close friends around for relief and support at the end of each day helped me truly get to the essence of this harrowing topic.

And, to the real heroes, the Holocaust survivors I am immensely fortunate to have been able to develop a deep connection with—no words can thank you. Thank you for showing us what it is like to live life, to persevere, to inspire, to learn and to grow. This work is dedicated to you, and to every single survivor, as well as those who perished too suddenly as a result of pure hatred. May their memory be a blessing and may we continue to learn from, and share, every story.

Works Cited:

"Rabbi Who Fled Nazis Rejoices in Life Here," The Brooklyn Daily Eagle. Brooklyn, New York. December 13, 1947.

Address by Avner Shalev, Chairman of the Yad Vashem Directorate. Sixth International Conference on Holocaust Education. Yad Vashem, Jerusalem. July 10, 2008.

Arendt, Hannah. *Eichmann in Jerusalem: A Report on the Banality of Evil.* Viking Press. 1963. New York, New York.

Avner, Yehuda. *The Ambassador.* The Toby Press. September 1, 2015. New York, New York.

Bauer, Yehuda. *A History of the Holocaust.* Single Title Social Studies. Franklin Watts. September 1, 2002. London, United Kingdom.

Bauman, Zygmunt. *Modernity and the Holocaust.* Cornell University Press. February 23, 2011. Ithaca, New York.

Beckermann, Ruth. *Die papierene Briicke/Paper Bridge.* Camera Nurith Aviv. Montage Gertraud Luschutzky. 95 min., 16 mm. filmladen, 1987.

Berkovits, Eliezer. *Faith After the Holocaust.* KTAV Publishing House. 1973. Brooklyn, New York.

Burgess, John. "Holocaust Museum's Multimedia Experiment," The Washington Post. July 28, 1991.

Felsen, Irit. "Adult-Onset Trauma and Intergenerational Transmission: Integrating Empirical Data and Psychoanalytic Theory," *Psychoanalysis, Self and Context.* 12:60-77, 2017. Taylor and Francis Group, LLC. January 4, 2017.

Goldberger, Paul. "Architecture View: A Memorial Evokes Unspeakable Events with Dignity," The New York Times. April 30, 1989.

Hansen, Marcus Lee. *The Problem of the Third Generation Immigrant.* Augustana Historical Society. January 1, 1938. Rock Island, Illinois.

Halbrach, Maurice. *La mémoire Collective.* The University Press of France. 1967. Paris, France.

Harel, Dorit. *Dilemmas in designing the Yad Vashem Holocaust History Museum.* Yad Vashem Publications. March 15, 2010. Jerusalem, Israel.

Helmreich, William B. *Against All Odds: Holocaust Survivors and the Successful Lives They Made in America.* Simon and Schuster. 1992. New York, New York

Hirsch, Marianne. *The Generation of Postmemory: Writing and Visual Culture After the Holocaust.* Columbia University Press. June 2012. New York, New York.

Huyssen, Andreas. *Present Pasts: Urban Palimpsests and the Politics of Memory.* Stanford University Press. 2003. Palo Alto, California.

IHRA. "A Matter of Comparison: The Holocaust, Genocides and Crimes Against Humanity," Survey drafted by the Committee on the Holocaust, Genocides and Crimes against Humanity. April 2016.

IHRA. "History Never Repeats Itself, but Sometimes It Rhymes Comparing the Holocaust to different Atrocities," Working Paper drafted by the Committee on the Holocaust, Genocides and Crimes against Humanity. Adopted by Iasi Plenary, November 10, 2016.

Kahane-Nissenbaum, Melissa C., "Exploring Intergenerational Transmission Of Trauma In Third Generation Holocaust Survivors" (2011). Doctorate in Social Work (DSW) Dissertations. 16.

Kaplan, Brett. Routledge Research in Cultural and Media Studies (Book 29). *Landscapes of Holocaust Postmemory.* Routledge, July 26, 2010.

Kenan, Orna. Preface. Saul Friedlander. Between Memory and History: The Evolution of Israeli Historiography of the Holocaust, 1945-1961. Peter Lang Publishing, United States, New York, US.

Klein, Kerwin Lee. "On the Emergence of Memory in Historical Discourse." *Representations*. No. 69, Special Issue: Grounds for Remembering. University of California Press. 2000. Berkeley, California.

Krell, Robert. *Child Holocaust Survivors: Memories and Reflections.* Trafford Publishing. October 29, 2007. Bloomington, Indiana.

Levi, Primo. "Revisiting the Camps," in The Art of Memory. Page 185

Levi, Primo. *The Drowned and the Saved.* Guilio Einaudi. April 1986. Italy.

Mayer, Jessica Else. "Nathan Englander, Shalom Auslander and the appropriation of the Holocaust in contemporary Jewish American fiction," England. 2016

Milton, Sybil. *In Fitting Memory: The Art and Politics Of Holocaust Memorials*. Wayne State University Press, 2018.

Muschamp, Herbert. "Architecture View: Shaping a Monument to History," The New York Times. April 11, 1993.

Nietzsche, Frederick. *On the Advantages and Disadvantages of History for Life*. Hackett Classics. Hackett Publishing Company, Inc. June 15, 1980. Indianapolis, Indiana.

Nora, Pierre. "Between Memory and History: Les Lieux de Memoire," in *Representations 26*.

Ockman, Joan. *Moshe Safdie- The Architecture of Memory*. Yad Vashem Publications. November 14, 2006. Jerusalem, Israel.

Olick, Jeffrey K., Vinitzky-Seroussi, Vered and Levy, Daniel. *The Collective Memory Reader*. Oxford University Press. 2011. New York, New York.

Rosenbloom, Maria. Bearing Witness: Implications for Mental Health Theory and Practice. *Bearing Witness to the Holocaust*. Symposium Series

(Book 31). Berger, Alan L. Edwin Mellen Press. October 1, 1991. Lewiston, New York.

Roth, Philip, et al. *Eli, the Fanatic*. Kernerman Publications, 1975.

Rovner, Michal. "Living Landscape," permanent video installation. Holocaust History Museum of Yad Vashem. 2005. Jerusalem, Israel.

Schemo, Diana Jean. "A Place to Remember, To Touch the Unbearable," The New York Times. April 18, 1993.

Shalev, Avner. "Mission Statement." *Yad Vashem*, Yad Vashem: The World Holocaust Remembrance Center, 2018.

Siegal, Nina. "Anne Frank Who? Museums Combat Ignorance About the Holocaust." *The New York Times*, The New York Times Company, 21 Mar. 2017.

Sigward, Daniel. *Holocaust and Human Behavior*. Facing History and Ourselves, 2017.
Spring 1989. Pages 7-24

Srour, Cheri. "Rudolph Hoess: Death Dealer" 2013. Brooklyn, New York.

Steinitz, Lucy Y. Psycho-Social Effects Of The Holocaust On Aging Survivors And Their Families, Journal of Gerontological Social Work,4:3-4, 145-152. October 25, 2008.

United States Holocaust Memorial Museum Strategic Plan Summary 2013-2018. USHMM.

Will, George F. "The Stones of Treblinka Cry Out," The Washington Post. September 10,1989.

Yerushalmi, Yosef Haim. *Zakhor: Jewish History and Jewish Memory*. Samuel and Althea Stroum Lectures in Jewish Studies. University of Washington Press. April 1, 1996. Seattle, Washington.

About the Author:

Eden Mia Hoffman is a recent graduate of New York University's Gallatin School of Individualized Study. Her concentration is titled "Consuming and Conserving The Social in the Contemporary Digital Age" and it explores the intersection of business, politics, the philosophy of technology and the social sciences. Prior to her studies at NYU, Eden spent a year studying in Israel. During her first year at NYU, Eden became involved in a number of groups on campus, like TAMID at NYU, an apolitical areligious group on college campuses throughout the globe that develops the professional skills of undergraduate students through hands-on interaction with the Israeli economy. As the Vice-President of the group at NYU, she, along with 119 other fellows from varying campuses, spent the summer in Tel Aviv, Israel, interning and immersing themselves in the Israeli tech scene. During that time, Eden worked in cyber security, after participating in the first TAVtech Fellowship in January of that same year, which brought 20 students from Harvard and NYU to Israel to study computer coding, data science and entrepreneurship. Eden also spent a year serving the downtown Jewish students as a co-President of Chabad House Bowery. During the spring semester of her Junior year, Eden took a leave of absence from NYU to pursue an independent research project titled *"Understanding Genocide: Inter-generational Abstraction and Dilution Through Three Generations Grappling with the Holocaust"* for which she received a grant to conduct. Simultaneously, Eden worked in the media department of the Consulate General of Israel in New York and worked independently on her academic concentration. Subsequently, Eden was a fellow in the Simon Wiesenthal Government Advocacy Program, where she interned for a member of the NYS Assembly. In August of 2017 she was invited as an undergraduate student to the ISGAP-Oxford Summer Institute, where she, along with doctoral and post-doctoral scholars from around the world, studied issues of extremism through the lens of contemporary anti-semitism. Eden is an avid reader and writer, having been a reader at the Elizabeth Kaplan Literary Agency, an editor of Gallatin's *The Literacy Review*, a research intern at The Davis Firm, PLLC., and a writer for *The Morning Brew Daily*. This is her first published book.

Made in the USA
Middletown, DE
23 April 2019